Real Estate Market Trends

A Comprehensive Guide to Secrets Behind Real Estate Market Fluctuations

Nicolas Abernathy

Introduction

- Overview of Real Estate Market

- Importance of Understanding Market Trends

Chapter 1: Historical Context

- Evolution of Real Estate Markets

- Key Milestones and Influential Factors

Chapter 2: Economic Factors

- Interest Rates

- Inflation

- Employment Rates

- GDP Impact on Real Estate

Chapter 3: Demographic Shifts

- Population Trends

- Generational Preferences

- Urbanization vs. Suburban Trends

Chapter 4: Technology's Influence

Chapter 5: Regulatory Landscape

Chapter 6: Global Market Interconnectedness

Chapter 7: Market Psychology

Chapter 8: Case Studies

- Examining Past Market Fluctuations

- Learning from Success Stories

- Avoiding Pitfalls

Chapter 9: Forecasting Techniques

- Data Analytics in Real Estate

- Machine Learning Models

- Expert Opinions vs. Quantitative Analysis

Chapter 10: Adapting to Change

- Strategies for Navigating Market Shifts

- Building Resilience in Real Estate Investments

- Embracing Innovation

Conclusion

Introduction

Overview of Real Estate Market

The real estate market serves as a dynamic ecosystem where the exchange of properties, capital, and investments intertwine to create a complex network. In this section, we delve into the fundamental structures of the real estate market, exploring its multifaceted components.

1. Segments of the Real Estate Market
   - Residential, commercial, industrial, and retail sectors: Unraveling the nuances of each segment and their interplay in the broader market.

2. Participants in the Market

- Agents, buyers, sellers, investors, developers, and other stakeholders: Understanding the roles and interactions shaping the market dynamics.

3. Market Cycles

- Examining the cyclical nature of real estate markets, from periods of growth and stability to downturns and recovery phases.

4. Key Metrics

- Price-to-earnings ratios, vacancy rates, and other essential metrics: Illuminating the quantitative aspects that gauge market health.

5. Geographical Variances

- Regional disparities and the impact of location on property values: Unpacking the significance of geography in real estate.

Importance of Understanding Market Trends

Understanding the dynamic trends within the real estate market is paramount for various stakeholders, from individual homeowners to institutional investors. This section explores the critical reasons why comprehending market trends is a cornerstone of success in real estate.

1. Risk Mitigation

   - Anticipating market shifts helps in proactively managing risks associated with property investments, enabling stakeholders to make informed decisions.

2. Strategic Investment

- Identifying trends allows investors to strategically position themselves, aligning their portfolios with emerging opportunities and avoiding potential pitfalls.

3. Financial Planning

- For individuals, businesses, and institutions, grasping market trends aids in effective financial planning, ensuring optimal allocation of resources in the real estate sector.

4. Policy and Regulation Adaptation

- Knowledge of market trends enables policymakers and regulators to adapt regulations to changing market conditions, fostering a balanced and sustainable real estate environment.

5. Informed Decision-Making

- Buyers and sellers armed with insights into market trends make more informed decisions, optimizing their transactions for better outcomes.

In the subsequent chapters, we will delve deeper into the historical context, economic factors, and other influential aspects shaping real estate market trends, building upon this foundational understanding.

Chapter 1: Historical Context

Evolution of Real Estate Markets

The evolution of real estate markets spans centuries, reflecting the intricate dance between societal, economic, and technological forces. This historical journey lays the groundwork for comprehending the contemporary landscape of property transactions and investments.

1. Ancient Foundations

   - Examining early forms of property ownership and land use in ancient civilizations, showcasing the rudimentary origins of real estate markets.

2. Feudal Systems to Private Ownership

- Tracing the transition from feudal land systems to the establishment of private property ownership, a pivotal shift that laid the groundwork for modern real estate.

3. Industrial Revolution Impact

- Analyzing how the Industrial Revolution triggered urbanization, leading to the rise of cities and the need for structured real estate markets to accommodate the growing population.

4. Post-World War Developments

- Exploring the impact of World Wars on global real estate, including the post-war housing boom and the emergence of suburban living.

5. Globalization and Market Integration

- Investigating how globalization facilitated the integration of real estate markets on a global scale, fostering cross-border investments and influencing market dynamics.

Key Milestones and Influential Factors

Real estate markets have been shaped by pivotal milestones and influential factors that have left an indelible mark on their trajectory. Understanding these key moments provides insights into the patterns and trends that continue to define the real estate landscape.

1. Great Depression
   - Analyzing the profound impact of the Great Depression on real estate markets, marked by

widespread foreclosures, declining property values, and a paradigm shift in regulatory frameworks.

2. Suburbanization Boom

- Investigating the post-World War II suburbanization trend, exploring the rise of suburban communities and the subsequent impact on housing demand and development.

3. Technology Revolution

- Examining how technological advancements, from the advent of the internet to PropTech innovations, have reshaped the way real estate transactions are conducted and properties are marketed.

4. Housing Bubble and Financial Crisis

- Delving into the causes and consequences of the housing bubble and financial crisis of the early 21st century, a period that highlighted vulnerabilities within real estate markets.

5. Sustainable Development Movement

- Exploring the influence of the sustainable development movement on real estate, including the growing emphasis on environmentally conscious and socially responsible practices.

Understanding the historical evolution and key milestones of real estate markets lays the groundwork for a nuanced exploration of the factors influencing market fluctuations, as we navigate through the pages of this comprehensive guide.

Chapter 2: Economic Factors

Interest Rates

Interest rates wield a profound influence on the real estate market, acting as a pivotal economic factor that shapes investment decisions, property values, and overall market dynamics.

1. Borrowing Costs and Affordability

   - Examining the direct correlation between interest rates and borrowing costs, and how fluctuations impact the affordability of mortgages, thereby influencing demand.

2. Investor Behavior

   - Analyzing how changes in interest rates alter the behaviour of real estate investors, including shifts in investment strategies, risk tolerance, and asset allocation.

3. Impact on Property Values

- Exploring the inverse relationship between interest rates and property values, as lower rates generally stimulate demand and lead to upward pressure on real estate prices.

4. Mortgage Market Dynamics

- Investigating the interplay between interest rates and the mortgage market, including the role of central banks in setting rates and the subsequent ripple effects on lending institutions and consumers.

B. Inflation

Inflation, as a measure of the general increase in prices over time, plays a crucial role in shaping the landscape of real estate markets and influencing investor decisions.

1. Preservation of Real Value

   - Analyzing how real estate, as a tangible asset, serves as a hedge against inflation by preserving its real value over the long term compared to cash or financial assets.

2. Cost of Construction and Development

   - Examining the impact of inflation on construction costs, influencing the feasibility and profitability of real estate development projects.

3. Rent and Income Dynamics

   - Investigating how inflation affects rental income and tenant affordability, as changes in the cost of living directly impact housing expenses.

4. Interest Rates and Inflation Link

- Understanding the intricate relationship between inflation and interest rates, and how central banks navigate this delicate balance to maintain economic stability.

Employment Rates

The employment landscape is a critical economic factor that reverberates throughout the real estate market, influencing both residential and commercial sectors.

1. Income Levels and Housing Demand

- Exploring the connection between employment rates, income levels, and the demand for housing, as job stability directly impacts individuals' ability to enter the real estate market.

2. Commercial Real Estate Impact
    - Analyzing the correlation between employment rates and the demand for commercial spaces, as thriving businesses contribute to a buoyant commercial real estate sector.

3. Geographical Employment Shifts
   - Investigating how changes in employment patterns, such as remote work trends, influence regional real estate markets and urban-suburban dynamics.

GDP Impact on Real Estate

The Gross Domestic Product (GDP) serves as a barometer of a nation's economic health, and its fluctuations have far-reaching implications for the real estate sector.

1. Economic Growth and Property Values

   - Examining the positive correlation between GDP growth and property values, as a robust economy often leads to increased consumer confidence and investment.

2. Commercial Real Estate Performance

   - Analyzing how GDP impacts the performance of the commercial real estate sector, with expanding economies driving demand for office, retail, and industrial spaces.

3. Government Policies and Stimulus

- Investigating how governments use fiscal and monetary policies to stimulate GDP growth, and the subsequent effects on real estate markets through increased investment and consumer spending.

4. Recessionary Effects

- Understanding how economic downturns, reflected in GDP contractions, can lead to challenges such as decreased property values, increased foreclosures, and a contraction in real estate development.

A comprehensive grasp of these economic factors provides a solid foundation for navigating the intricate terrain of real estate market trends and fluctuations. In the subsequent chapters, we will further explore demographic shifts, technological influences, and regulatory landscapes that contribute to the ever-evolving nature of the real estate market.

Chapter 3: Demographic Shifts

Population Trends

Understanding population trends is a fundamental aspect of deciphering the dynamics of the real estate market. The ebb and flow of population growth and distribution have profound implications for housing demand, urban planning, and regional development.

1. Population Growth and Housing Demand

- Analyzing how increasing populations contribute to rising demand for housing, impacting both residential and commercial real estate markets.

2. Age Distribution

- Examining the age composition of a population and its influence on housing needs, from the demand for starter homes by young adults to the preferences of seniors for retirement communities.

3. Migration Patterns

- Investigating how internal and external migration patterns shape real estate markets, with cities experiencing population influxes often facing increased demand and rising property values.

4. Impacts on Infrastructure

- Exploring the challenges and opportunities posed by population growth on infrastructure development, including transportation, utilities, and public services.

Generational Preferences

The preferences of different generations play a pivotal role in shaping real estate trends, from housing styles to neighborhood choices and amenities.

1. Baby Boomers

   - Analyzing the housing preferences of baby boomers, including downsizing trends, the demand for age-friendly features, and the rise of active adult communities.

2. Generation X

   - Examining how Generation X influences real estate markets, from their emphasis on work-life balance to preferences for suburban living and family-friendly neighborhoods.

3. Millennials

- Investigating the impact of millennials on housing markets, exploring trends such as delayed homeownership, urban living preferences, and the demand for technology-integrated homes.

4. Gen Z

- Anticipating the emerging trends driven by Gen Z, including their tech-savvy preferences, environmental consciousness, and potential shifts in housing choices.

Urbanization vs. Suburban Trends

The ongoing tug-of-war between urban and suburban living preferences significantly shapes real estate landscapes, influencing everything from property values to infrastructure development.

1. Urban Renaissance

   - Analyzing the resurgence of urban living, exploring factors such as walkability, access to cultural amenities, and the appeal of city centers for certain demographics.

2. Suburban Resurgence

   - Examining the renewed interest in suburban living, driven by factors like affordability, larger living spaces, and the rise of remote work facilitating a shift away from city centers.

3. Transit-Oriented Development

- Investigating how urban and suburban areas are adapting to the demand for transit-oriented developments, integrating public transportation options with residential and commercial spaces.

4. Impact on Commercial Real Estate

- Exploring how demographic shifts influence the demand for commercial spaces, from the rise of co-working spaces in urban centers to the transformation of suburban malls into mixed-use developments.

Understanding the intricate interplay of population trends, generational preferences, and urbanization versus suburbanization dynamics is essential for stakeholders navigating the evolving real estate landscape. In the subsequent sections, we will delve into the technological advancements influencing the market and the regulatory frameworks that shape real estate transactions.

Chapter 4: Technology's Influence

PropTech Innovations

The marriage of technology and real estate, often termed PropTech, has revolutionized the industry, introducing innovations that redefine how properties are bought, sold, and managed.

1. Smart Homes and IoT Integration

   - Exploring the integration of Internet of Things (IoT) devices in homes, enhancing efficiency, security, and energy management.

2. Blockchain in Real Estate Transactions

   - Analyzing the potential of blockchain technology in streamlining and securing property transactions, from title transfers to smart contracts.

3. Augmented and Virtual Reality (AR/VR)

- Examining how AR and VR technologies are transforming the real estate experience, enabling virtual property tours, interactive design previews, and immersive marketing.

4. Data Analytics and Predictive Modeling

- Investigating how data analytics and predictive modelling empower real estate professionals with insights into market trends, pricing strategies, and investment opportunities.

5. Crowdfunding Platforms

- Exploring the rise of crowdfunding platforms in real estate, allowing a broader range of investors to participate in projects and fostering a more democratized investment landscape.

Virtual Real Estate Trends

The virtual realm has become an integral part of the real estate landscape, shaping how properties are showcased, evaluated, and transacted.

1. Virtual Property Tours

   - Analyzing the impact of virtual property tours, providing prospective buyers with immersive experiences and the ability to explore homes remotely.

2. Digital Twins and 3D Modeling

- Examining the use of digital twins and 3D modelling in real estate, facilitating more accurate property representations and aiding in architectural planning.

3. Blockchain for Virtual Land Ownership

- Investigating the emergence of virtual real estate on blockchain platforms, where users can buy, sell, and own digital land and assets within virtual environments.

4. Metaverse Integration

- Exploring how the metaverse is influencing real estate, with virtual worlds becoming spaces for social interaction, commerce, and even virtual real estate development.

Impact of Digital Marketing

Digital marketing has become a powerful tool in the real estate industry, reshaping how properties are marketed, and how buyers and sellers connect.

1. Online Listing Platforms

- Analyzing the dominance of online listing platforms, such as Zillow and Realtor.com, in reshaping how properties are marketed and discovered.

2. Social Media Marketing

- Examining the role of social media in real estate marketing, from targeted advertising on platforms like Facebook to influencer collaborations and community engagement.

3. Search Engine Optimization (SEO) for Real Estate

- Investigating the importance of SEO in real estate marketing, ensuring properties and real estate services are discoverable in online searches.

4. Virtual Staging and Digital Content Creation

- Exploring the use of virtual staging and digital content creation to enhance property images and create compelling visual narratives in marketing materials.

The fusion of technology and real estate is an ongoing journey, continually reshaping how the industry operates. In the subsequent sections, we will explore the regulatory frameworks impacting real estate and delve into the interconnectedness of global markets.

Chapter 5: Regulatory Landscape

Government policies, zoning regulations, and taxation play pivotal roles in shaping the real estate sector, creating the legal and administrative framework that governs property transactions, land development, and fiscal considerations.

Government Policies

Government policies wield significant influence over the real estate market, serving as both catalysts for growth and safeguards against instability.

- Housing Policies: Examining government initiatives aimed at promoting affordable housing, homeownership, and addressing housing shortages.

- Interest Rate and Monetary Policies: Analyzing the impact of central bank decisions on interest rates, influencing borrowing costs and mortgage rates.

- Economic Stimulus Programs: Investigating how government-led stimulus programs can boost the real estate sector during economic downturns, with measures like tax incentives and subsidies.

Zoning and Land Use Regulations

Zoning and land use regulations are critical tools employed by governments to manage urban development, preserve natural resources, and maintain the character of communities.

- Residential Zoning: Exploring regulations that govern the types of residential structures allowed in specific zones, influencing the density and character of neighbourhoods.

- Commercial and Industrial Zoning: Analyzing how zoning regulations shape the locations and types of businesses allowed in different areas, impacting the economic landscape.

- Mixed-Use Developments: Examining the rise of mixed-use zoning, where areas accommodate a blend of residential, commercial, and recreational spaces to create vibrant, interconnected communities.

Taxation Impact on Real Estate

Taxation policies have far-reaching implications for real estate, influencing investment decisions, property values, and overall market stability.

- Property Taxes: Analyzing the role of property taxes in municipal revenue generation and their impact on homeowners, businesses, and local governments.

- Capital Gains Taxes: Examining how capital gains taxes affect real estate transactions, influencing investor behaviour and the timing of property sales.

- Tax Incentives for Real Estate Development: Investigating government initiatives that provide tax incentives to spur development in specific regions or for certain types of projects.

- Foreign Investment Taxes: Exploring how governments regulate and tax foreign investments in real estate, aiming to balance economic growth with concerns about affordability and market stability.

Understanding and navigating the regulatory landscape is crucial for all participants in the real estate market, from individual homeowners to developers and investors. In the subsequent chapters, we will explore the interconnectedness of global real estate markets and delve into the psychological aspects influencing market behaviour.

Chapter 6: Global Market Interconnectedness

The real estate market has become increasingly interconnected on a global scale, influenced by international investments, cross-border trends, and geopolitical factors. This interconnectedness introduces both opportunities and challenges that shape the dynamics of real estate markets worldwide.

1. International Investments

Real estate has become a favoured asset class for international investors seeking diversification and long-term growth. Understanding the patterns of international investments is crucial in deciphering the global interconnectedness of real estate markets.

- Foreign Direct Investment (FDI): Analyzing how FDI flows into real estate, exploring the motivations behind cross-border investments and their impact on local property markets.

- Global Real Estate Funds: Examining the rise of global real estate funds, enabling investors to participate in diverse property portfolios across different countries and regions.

- Sovereign Wealth Funds: Investigating the role of sovereign wealth funds in real estate investments, often playing a significant part in shaping the global landscape.

2. Cross-Border Real Estate Trends

The movement of capital, businesses, and individuals across borders has given rise to distinct cross-border trends in real estate, influencing property values, market demand, and development strategies.

- Global Cities and Hubs: Exploring the emergence of global cities and hubs that attract cross-border investments, driven by factors such as economic stability, cultural appeal, and business opportunities.

- International Commercial Real Estate: Analyzing trends in international commercial real estate, including the expansion of multinational corporations, co-working spaces, and the globalization of retail and hospitality sectors.

- Residential Real Estate Trends: Examining how cross-border trends affect residential real estate, from the rise of luxury global real estate markets to the impact on local housing affordability.

3. Geopolitical Factors

Geopolitical events and dynamics have a profound impact on global real estate markets, introducing uncertainties and influencing investment decisions.

- Political Stability and Investment: Analyzing how political stability or instability in different regions affects investor confidence and influences real estate investment strategies.

- Trade Relations: Investigating the impact of trade relations and tariff policies on cross-border real estate transactions, particularly in regions with strong economic ties.

- Global Economic Shifts: Exploring how global economic shifts, such as the rise of emerging markets or economic downturns in major economies, influence real estate investment patterns.

Understanding the intricate web of international investments, cross-border trends, and geopolitical factors is essential for real estate professionals, investors, and policymakers to navigate the complexities of a globally interconnected market. In the subsequent chapters, we will delve into the psychological aspects of market behaviour and explore forecasting techniques to anticipate and adapt to changes in the real estate landscape.

Chapter 7: Market Psychology

Market psychology is a powerful force shaping real estate trends, driven by investor sentiment, behavioural economics, and media influence. Understanding these psychological aspects is paramount for participants in the real estate market.

Investor Sentiment

Investor sentiment, the collective mood and perception of market participants, plays a crucial role in determining market movements and trends.

1. Fear and Greed Dynamics

- Analyzing how fear and greed influence investor decisions, impacting buying and selling patterns in real estate markets.

2. Risk Aversion vs. Risk Appetite

- Examining the delicate balance between risk aversion and risk appetite, as investors navigate uncertainties in the real estate landscape.

3. Herding Behavior

- Investigating the phenomenon of herding behaviour, where investors follow the crowd, often amplifying market movements and trends.

4. Impact of Market News and Events

- Analyzing how breaking news, economic indicators, and geopolitical events shape investor sentiment, leading to shifts in real estate market dynamics.

Behavioral Economics in Real Estate

Behavioural economics explores how psychological factors influence economic decision-making, offering insights into the irrational behaviours that impact real estate markets.

1. Anchoring and Pricing Decisions

   - Examining how anchoring, or fixating on specific price points, influences both buyers and sellers in real estate transactions.

2. Loss Aversion

   - Analyzing the concept of loss aversion and its impact on decision-making, as individuals may be more motivated to avoid losses than to secure gains in real estate investments.

3. Cognitive Biases in Decision-Making

   - Investigating common cognitive biases, such as confirmation bias and availability heuristics, and their role in shaping perceptions and choices in the real estate market.

4. Prospect Theory in Real Estate

   - Exploring how prospect theory, which describes how people make decisions under uncertainty, is manifested in real estate investment choices.

Media Influence on Market Perception

Media, including traditional outlets and social platforms, holds significant sway over market perceptions, influencing how participants view and engage with real estate opportunities.

1. Sensationalism and Market Hype

- Analyzing the impact of sensationalized reporting and market hype on investor behaviour, potentially leading to speculative bubbles and sudden market shifts.

2. Role of Social Media

- Examining the role of social media platforms in shaping real estate trends, from viral property listings to the amplification of market sentiment.

3. Expert Opinions and Commentary

- Investigating how expert opinions and commentary in media outlets can shape investor sentiment, influencing decisions ranging from buying/selling choices to investment strategies.

4. Market Narratives

- Exploring the creation and propagation of market narratives through media channels, which contribute to the overall perception of market conditions.

Understanding the psychological underpinnings of investor sentiment, behavioural economics, and media influence is crucial for market participants seeking to navigate the nuanced and often unpredictable terrain of the real estate market. In the subsequent chapters, we will delve into case studies, forecasting techniques, and strategies for adapting to market changes.

Chapter 8: Case Studies

Real-world case studies provide valuable insights into the intricacies of past market fluctuations, success stories, and cautionary tales, offering a practical lens through which to understand the dynamics of the real estate market.

Examining Past Market Fluctuations

1. The 2008 Financial Crisis

   - Analyzing the causes and effects of the 2008 financial crisis on the real estate market, exploring the role of subprime mortgages, housing bubbles, and regulatory responses.

2. Post-Recession Recovery in the U.S.

- Examining how the U.S. real estate market rebounded after the 2008 recession, highlighting factors such as government interventions, low interest rates, and the resilience of certain regional markets.

3. Global Financial Crises and Real Estate

- Investigating how real estate markets globally have responded to various financial crises, considering regional variations and the role of economic interconnectedness.

4. Impact of COVID-19 on Real Estate

- Analyzing the effects of the COVID-19 pandemic on the real estate market, including shifts in demand for remote work-friendly properties, changes in urban-suburban dynamics, and the resilience of certain sectors.

Learning from Success Stories

1. Urban Revitalization Projects

- Exploring successful urban revitalization projects that transformed blighted areas into thriving neighbourhoods, examining the key factors that contributed to their success.

2. Adaptive Reuse and Redevelopment

- Examining cases of adaptive reuse and redevelopment, where existing structures are repurposed for new uses, showcasing the economic and cultural benefits of such initiatives.

3. Strategic Investment Portfolios

- Analyzing the success stories of investors who strategically built diversified portfolios, exploring how a mix of property types and locations contributed to their long-term success.

4. Public-Private Partnerships (PPPs)

- Investigating cases where public-private partnerships played a pivotal role in successful real estate projects, highlighting the collaborative efforts between government entities and private developers.

Avoiding Pitfalls

1. Overleveraging and Debt

- Examining cases where overleveraging and excessive debt led to financial distress, emphasizing the importance of prudent financial management in real estate investments.

2. Failure of Due Diligence

- Analyzing instances where insufficient due diligence resulted in unforeseen challenges, emphasizing the need for thorough research and risk assessment before making real estate decisions.

3. Market Timing Mistakes

- Investigating cases where poor market timing negatively impacted investment returns, highlighting the challenges of accurately predicting market cycles and the importance of a long-term perspective.

4. Regulatory Compliance Issues

- Examining cases where regulatory compliance issues led to legal complications and financial losses, underscoring the significance of staying informed about and adhering to relevant regulations.

Case studies serve as invaluable tools for learning from both the successes and failures of others in the real estate arena. In the subsequent chapters, we will explore forecasting techniques and strategies for adapting to changes in the real estate landscape.

Chapter 9: Forecasting Techniques

Accurate forecasting is a cornerstone of successful real estate decision-making. In this section, we explore various forecasting techniques, including the role of data analytics, machine learning models, and the balance between expert opinions and quantitative analysis.

Data Analytics in Real Estate

1. Market Trends Analysis
   - Utilizing historical data to identify and analyze long-term and short-term trends in the

real estate market, providing insights into potential future movements.

2. Predictive Modeling

- Employing statistical models to predict future market conditions, incorporating factors such as economic indicators, demographic trends, and property-specific variables.

3. Demand-Supply Dynamics

- Analyzing data on current and projected supply and demand for real estate in specific regions, helping to anticipate potential imbalances and market fluctuations.

4. Price Index Analysis

- Utilizing price indices to track changes in property values over time, aiding in the identification of market trends and the assessment of potential investment opportunities.

Machine Learning Models

1. Price Prediction Models

- Implementing machine learning algorithms to predict future property prices, taking into account a range of variables such as location, economic indicators, and historical price trends.

2. Risk Assessment Models

- Developing models that assess and quantify risks associated with real estate investments, incorporating factors like market volatility, economic stability, and regulatory changes.

3. Sentiment Analysis

- Leveraging natural language processing and sentiment analysis to gauge market sentiment from online sources, news articles, and social media, providing additional insights into investor perceptions.

4. Property Valuation Models

- Using machine learning to enhance property valuation accuracy by considering a broader set of features and comparing them to recent comparable sales.

Expert Opinions vs. Quantitative Analysis

1. Expert Opinions

- Assessing the role of expert opinions in real estate forecasting, recognizing the value of industry expertise, market insights, and qualitative assessments.

2. Quantitative Analysis

- Emphasizing the importance of quantitative analysis in supplementing expert opinions, providing a data-driven foundation for decision-making and risk management.

3. Integration of Both Approaches

- Recognizing the complementary nature of expert opinions and quantitative analysis, suggesting an integrated approach where qualitative insights are validated and enriched by quantitative data.

4. Challenges and Pitfalls

- Highlighting the potential challenges and pitfalls associated with overreliance on either expert opinions or quantitative analysis alone, emphasizing the need for a balanced and holistic forecasting approach.

By combining data analytics, machine learning models, and expert opinions, real estate professionals can build robust forecasting strategies that adapt to the dynamic nature of the market. In the subsequent chapters, we will explore strategies for adapting to market shifts and building resilience in real estate investments.

Chapter 10: Adapting to Change

The ability to adapt to change is a crucial aspect of navigating the ever-evolving landscape of the real estate market. This section explores strategies for effectively responding to market shifts, building resilience in investments, and embracing innovation.

Strategies for Navigating Market Shifts

1. Diversification of Portfolios
   - Advocating for a diversified portfolio that spans different property types, locations, and

investment strategies, reducing vulnerability to specific market fluctuations.

2. Market Research and Continuous Learning

- Emphasizing the importance of staying informed through continuous market research, monitoring trends, and adapting strategies based on evolving economic, demographic, and regulatory factors.

3. Agile Decision-Making

- Encouraging an agile decision-making approach, allowing investors and stakeholders to swiftly respond to changing market conditions and capitalize on emerging opportunities.

4. Flexibility in Financing

- Promoting flexible financing structures that can adapt to varying interest rates, economic climates, and financing options, providing resilience during market uncertainties.

Building Resilience in Real Estate Investments

1. Stress Testing Portfolios

   - Advocating for stress testing investment portfolios to assess their resilience to adverse market conditions, helping investors identify potential vulnerabilities and implement risk mitigation measures.

2. Sustainable and Adaptive Design

   - Encouraging the incorporation of sustainable and adaptive design principles in real estate projects, enhancing their ability to withstand environmental changes and market fluctuations.

3. Long-Term Investment Perspective

- Promoting a long-term investment perspective, acknowledging that real estate values may experience short-term fluctuations but historically tend to appreciate over extended periods.

4. Risk Management Strategies

- Implementing comprehensive risk management strategies, including insurance coverage, contingency planning, and hedging mechanisms to mitigate potential financial losses.

Embracing Innovation

1. Technology Integration

- Encouraging the adoption of PropTech innovations to streamline processes, enhance efficiency, and improve the overall performance of real estate portfolios.

2. Innovative Financing Models

- Exploring and embracing innovative financing models, such as crowdfunding and blockchain-based transactions, to diversify funding sources and increase accessibility.

3. Environmental, Social, and Governance (ESG) Practices

- Emphasizing the integration of ESG practices in real estate investments, meeting the growing demand for socially responsible and sustainable development.

4. Adapting to Changing Demographics

- Recognizing and adapting to changing demographic trends, such as the rise of remote work and preferences for sustainable and community-oriented living.

By incorporating these strategies, investors, developers, and other stakeholders can navigate market shifts, build resilience in their real estate investments, and embrace innovation to stay at the forefront of industry trends. In the subsequent chapters, we will summarize key insights and explore future trends in the ever-evolving real estate market.

Conclusion

Summarizing Key Insights

In this comprehensive guide, we embarked on a journey through the multifaceted realms of the real estate market. Here are the key insights gleaned from our exploration:

1. Understanding Market Fundamentals

   - Recognizing the foundational elements of real estate, from market structures and property types to the intricate web of economic, demographic, and regulatory factors shaping the industry.

2. Navigating Historical Context

- Delving into the historical evolution of real estate markets, unravelling the key milestones, and understanding the factors that have influenced the ebb and flow of property transactions over centuries.

3. Economic Forces at Play

- Grasping the intricate dance between economic factors and real estate, from interest rates and inflation to the profound impact of GDP growth on property values.

4. Demographic Shifts and Urban Dynamics

- Exploring the nuances of demographic trends, generational preferences, and the ongoing tug-of-war between urbanization and suburbanization shaping real estate landscapes.

5. Technological Transformations

- Unveiling the profound influence of technology on real estate, from PropTech innovations and virtual real estate trends to the evolving landscape of digital marketing.

6. Navigating the Regulatory Landscape

- Understanding the critical role of government policies, zoning regulations, and taxation in shaping the legal and administrative framework of real estate transactions.

7. Global Market Interconnectedness

- Acknowledging the interconnected nature of global real estate markets, examining the impact of international investments, cross-border trends, and geopolitical factors.

8. Market Psychology Unveiled

- Peeling back the layers of market psychology, from investor sentiment and behavioural economics to the influence of media on market perceptions.

9. Learning from Case Studies

- Drawing lessons from real-world cases, both successes and pitfalls, to gain practical insights into the dynamics of real estate decision-making.

10. Forecasting Techniques for Strategic Planning

- Unraveling the intricacies of forecasting, exploring the role of data analytics, machine learning models, and the balance between expert opinions and quantitative analysis.

11. Adapting to Change

- Equipping ourselves with strategies to navigate market shifts, build resilience in real estate investments, and embrace innovation in the face of a dynamic and evolving industry.

Looking Ahead: Future Trends in Real Estate

1. Sustainable Development

- Anticipating a continued emphasis on sustainable and environmentally conscious development practices, driven by increased awareness and regulatory pressures.

2. PropTech Evolution

- Watching the evolution of PropTech with keen interest, as technologies like artificial intelligence, blockchain, and augmented reality reshape the way real estate is transacted and managed.

3. Flexible Workspaces

- Acknowledging the lasting impact of remote work on real estate, with a shift toward flexible workspaces, co-living arrangements, and adaptive use of commercial properties.

4. Smart Cities and IoT Integration

- Envisioning the continued integration of smart city initiatives and IoT technologies, enhancing urban living experiences and the efficiency of infrastructure.

5. Globalization and Investment Opportunities

- Expecting increased globalization of real estate investment opportunities, with investors exploring diverse markets and cross-border collaborations becoming more prevalent.

6. Affordable Housing Solutions

   - Recognizing the growing need for innovative solutions to address affordable housing challenges, with a focus on inclusive and community-centric development.

7. Resilience and Risk Management

   - Emphasizing the importance of resilience and risk management in real estate, with stakeholders incorporating adaptive design, sustainable practices, and robust risk assessment into their strategies.

As we conclude this comprehensive guide, the real estate landscape stands as a dynamic canvas, shaped by a myriad of factors and constantly evolving. Armed with insights and strategies, stakeholders can navigate the challenges and seize the opportunities presented by this ever-changing industry.